A Caregiver's Journal

Recording Lessons of Love and Hope

Christine Green

A Caregiver's Journal

Recording Lessons of Love and Hope

Christine Green

WiseWoman Press

A Caregiver's Journal: Recording Lessons of Love and Hope

Managing Editor: Michael Terranova

ISBN: 978-0-945385-45-5
WiseWoman Press
Portland, OR 97217

www.wisewomanpress.com

Spirituality/self-help/health, mind and body

Also by the author

Anatomy of Caring:
Insights on faith from a caregiver and a patient

Authentic Spirituality:
A Woman's Guide to Living an Empowered Life

Dedicated to caregivers

and their loved ones

Contents

Introduction.. 11
Who Cares? 14
Detour of Faith 16
Giving Love 18
Advice.. 20
Support 22
A Good Report.. 24
Patients Have Patience 26
The Bracelet.. 28
Faith is Freedom 30
Peaceful Sleep 32
Walk in Faith 34
One Day at a Time 36
Helplessness 38
Waiting...40
Standing in Faith.. 42
Visualizing Love 44
Medicine Comes from God 46
Change is Constant..48
Asking Questions..50
Realization of Loss 52
Back to the Basics...54
The Economics of Illness...56
No Small Steps...58
Speech Therapy 60
Unexpected Gifts 62
Beams of Love 64
Treats 66
Pain Relief 68
Army of Angels 70
Trust 72
Gratitude 74

Navigator 76
Be Kind to Caregivers 78
Faith.. 80
A Caregiver's Prayer 82
Worry 84
Letting Go 86
Move Mountains 88
Expectations 90
Never Alone 92
Bible References... 95
Caregiving Resources 97
About the Author 99

Introduction

This book is probably in your hands because you are a caregiver. Someone close to you is no longer able to care for themselves and you were chosen or volunteered to be their caregiver and advocate.

I thought I understood caregiving until I cared for my husband Laurence during his long illness.* I was humbled realizing the walk of faith necessary along with unlimited patience and unconditional love.

I come from a family of caregivers. My Dad was one of the oldest of 12 children and he left high school to get a job so he could help support his family. In the 1960's my grandfather suffered a number of strokes and was unable to walk. He weighed over 200 pounds and my grandmother wasn't strong enough to move him. For 10 years, my mother went to their home every night and put my grandfather to bed and each morning she got him up and dressed and sat him in his chair. My sister cared for my Mom after a heart attack both at home and in a nursing home. Now she cares for my Dad who lives home alone.

Caregiving is complex. It demands us to be patient, strong, persistent, fearless and gentle. We are called on to be advocates, listeners, errand-runners and negotiators while dealing with our own feelings of guilt, failure, disappointment and fear. At the same time we do our best to take care of ourselves so we can care for others.

And yet in the midst of pain, fear and sorrow, the opportunity to be a caregiver is truly a gift. The time we spend with our loved ones is precious. There is an awareness of love that is amazingly profound.

My intention is that this journal will be your companion as you spend time waiting, worrying and wondering about your loved one. I hope you will use it to record the fleeting joys and profound struggles of caregiving. I hope you will find a story that reminds you that you are not alone and that you gain some inspiration that gives you hope on the tough days.

I would be honored to hear how you used this book and all that you learned from your own caregiving experience. Please email me at revgreen@sacredheartministries.org

Please know that you are blessed beyond measure for your gracious giving. May God's grace guide you with love.

*A more detailed version of my caregiving experience can be found in, Anatomy of Caring, Insights on faith from a caregiver and a patient. It is part journal and part memoir of my journey as a caregiver and includes Laurence's journal about his experience as a patient.

Who Cares?

Who cares? I do. And I know you do. We care because we love and we love because we care.

I absolutely know that God cares for us and loves us unconditionally. And just when we think we can't face another day, God sends us a caregiver to give us a call or a hug or lend a helping hand.

"No eye has seen, no ear has heard, and no mind has imagined what God has prepared for those who love Him."

1 Corinthians 2:9

Praise God.

What challenge am I willing to turn over to God?

For nothing is impossible with God. Luke 1:37 (NIV)

Detour of Faith

I was very prepared for the New Year. I cleaned out the garage, organized my office, upgraded my computer and was ready to take on the year. There is a saying, "Life happens when we are making other plans." My husband Laurence had developed blood clots in his hands that caused intense piercing pain. His doctors scrambled to find the cause and to relieve the pain.

I had to pull on everything I had ever taught about faith. Instead of being the teacher, I became the student taking notes about life, faith, prayer.

Perspective of life changes so quickly. Things that would normally send me into frenzy suddenly seemed harmless. I developed a great compassion for anyone with health issues or dealing with pain. I had a profound appreciation for the dozens and dozens of people who offered to pray.

In healing there are so many hurdles and obstacles to overcome. It became important to remember to keep the faith.

I am willing to turn to faith today.

_____

_____

_____

_____

_____

_____

_____

_____

_____

_____

_____

_____

_____

_____

_____

_____

The mind of man plans his way, but the Lord directs his steps.
Proverbs 16:9 (NASB)

Giving Love

Spending time with a loved one in the hospital you have the opportunity to see other families and all that they are going through. Each one of us has our own story and our own challenges.

I took the time to talk with another wife caring for her husband. I listened to the pain in her voice. I could relate to her anxiety.

It doesn't take much energy to listen. It means so much for the person in pain.

The more love you give out, the more you get back in return.

I am so grateful God is so gracious.

Where can I express more love today?

And we know that in all things God works for the good of those who love him, who have been called according to his purpose. Romans 8:28 (NIV)

Advice

We want to help. We are sincere in caring for each other and want to do what we can. So we shower the caregiver with good ideas: try these vitamins, lotions, hot packs, cold packs, music, hot pepper and green tea.

While I usually appreciated the concern and the ideas, I was mostly left overwhelmed. There was one more thing to do, another topic to research, and one more decision to make.

Prayer is the most powerful gift. But it sometimes is a difficult gift to give. It requires us to face our beliefs and tackle our faith. It can seem empty if we don't have a relationship with God. Prayer can feel inadequate because we didn't "do" something. Our ego definitely wants to take action and feel satisfied.

Prayer is humbling and powerful. It is an extraordinary gift.

Lord, hear my prayer...

Therefore I tell you, whatever you ask for in prayer, believe that you have received it, and it will be yours. Mark 11:24 (NIV)

Support

The patient's request for privacy is understandable. However, it can be challenging for the caregiver.

An important part of being a caregiver is to build a support network. Help with doctor visits, home cooked meals, and groceries delivered are life-savers for both the caregiver and patient. I learned to open the door and let others in.

As it turned out, friends thanked me for letting them be part of the healing process.

Praise God.

What support would I like to receive?

So I say to you: Ask and it will be given to you; seek and you will find, knock and the door will be opened to you. For everyone who asks receives; he who seeks finds; and to him who knocks, the door will be opened.
Luke 11:9-10 (NIV)

A Good Report

The healing process is overwhelming. There is so much to take in each day. We learned to acknowledge and give thanks for each good report received along the way.

Stable platelet counts, steady lab reports, and positive doctor updates were good reports we learned to appreciate.

Thank you God for good reports.

What I am grateful for today?

_No eye has seen, no ear has heard, no mind has conceived what God has
prepared for those who love him._ 1 Corinthians 2:9 (NIV)

Patients Have Patience

One particular doctor appointment found us waiting for an hour for the oncologist, only to find that he wanted Laurence to see another specialist, who was in another building on the campus. Finally the specialist arrived and examined Laurence and gave him a good report.

We were left waiting, again, for the oncologist to return. As I paced back and forth in front of the room I smiled at a man who I knew had been waiting much longer than we had. I made a comment about always having to wait, and he calmly replied, "I guess that's why they call us patients."

All too true.

Where can I practice being more patient?

The Lord is my strength and my shield; my heart trusts in him and I am
helped. My heart leaps for joy and I will give thanks to him in song.
Psalm 28:7 (NIV)

The Bracelet

While in Jerusalem on a pilgrimage, I had purchased a few bracelets at a little market to give as gifts. I kept a pink one for myself. It was a simple beaded bracelet, but it had meaning and memories.

One day, at a doctor visit with Laurence, I realized my bracelet was missing after we left the clinic. Going back to find it was not an option. I thought to myself, I am going to trust that my bracelet will be replaced. I don't know how or when but I know nothing is ever lost in God.

*The next day my friend Pam came to visit. As we were finishing lunch Pam pulled a little bag out of her purse and presented her handmade gift to me. Not one, not two, not three, but **seven** beautiful emerald green and sapphire blue beaded bracelets. My missing bracelet was returned within 24 hours. Multiplied. With Love.*

One of many signs and wonders that God so graciously provides. It was a reminder to me to let go and trust God for my good. My job is to stand in faith.

I am so grateful God is so gracious.

What I am standing in faith for today?

We throw open our doors to God and discover at the same moment that he has already thrown open his door to us. Romans 5:2 (MSG)

Faith is Freedom

In the past I would pray so that bad things wouldn't happen: Please deliver me from evil.

Truth is that life is messy. It's full of ups and down, struggles and triumphs, pain and freedom. As much as I would like to keep it neat and tidy, life seems to have a mind of its own. What I know is that sometimes the uncomfortable and painful experiences are the ones that open the door to freedom.

Faith is the freedom in knowing that whatever I need will be provided; whether it's having the strength to face the day, courage to speak my truth, or help for a loved one. Faith is appreciating every day as a treasure and every experience as a gift.

So it is written: "I know the plans I have for you declared the Lord, plans to prosper you and not harm you; plans to give you hope and a future." Jeremiah 29:11

And on this I place my faith.

I live in faith today despite what life looks like.

Give thanks to the Lord for he is good; his love endures forever.
Psalm 107:1 (NIV)

Peaceful Sleep

Laurence was resting at home after a week of chemo. I was sitting at my desk and chatting away to Laurence in the other room, only to walk in and find him sound asleep. I wish I could fall asleep so quickly.

Sleep is a precious commodity to the caregiver. Something we seem to lose the moment we take on the role of caregiver.

I learned over time that the less I stressed over the lack of sleep, the more peace I was able to maintain. The greater peace I felt, the greater my ability to function.

Praise God.

What challenges can I give to God so I can rest?

Peace I leave you; my peace I give you. I do not give to you as the world gives. Do not let your hearts be troubled and do not be afraid.
John 14:7 (NIV)

Walk in Faith

My friend was helping her mother care for her dad who has the beginning stages of Alzheimer's. She's shared about the struggles of looking after her parents, balancing caring for her family and keeping her business going.

And in the next breath she shared the joy, love and moments of laughter spending time with her dad.

That's what care givers do. We care. We give. We struggle. We fall down. We get up again.

It's all a walk of faith.

I put my faith in God's wisdom to guide me.

Give thanks to the Lord, for he is good; his love endures forever.
Psalm 118:1 (NIV)

One Day at a Time

I have learned so much through the process of being a caregiver: the practice of taking one day at a time, the power of prayer, the extraordinary healing presence of love.

There are many other phases to move through as a caregiver. We do our best to be grateful for what we have each day. I was always so grateful for the amazing prayer and love being sent our way.

God is truly gracious.

Today what is one thing I can accept as God's blessing?

_____

_____

_____

_____

_____

_____

_____

_____

_____

_____

_____

_____

_____

_____

_____

_____

Let the morning bring me word of your unfailing love, for I have put my trust in you. Psalm 143:8 (NIV)

Helplessness

Two steps forward, one step back. Sometimes three steps back. We learn how little control we actually have in life.

Some days it just feels like moving through mud. Pain, obstacles, set-backs can feel overwhelming.

I look back on those moments and know that prayers were keeping me going. There was only faith to rely on.

Lord, hear my prayer:

_____

_____

_____

_____

_____

_____

_____

_____

_____

_____

_____

_____

_____

_____

_____

_____

Though the mountains be shaken and the hills be removed, yet my unfailing love for you will not be shaken nor my covenant of peace be removed, says the Lord, who has compassion on you. Isaiah 54:10 (NIV)

Waiting

Waiting... waiting... waiting. Why do things take so long?

An enormous amount of time is spent waiting as a caregiver. We wait for the doctor, a new report, something to change, or our beloved to wake up. Our brains are mush and nerves are frayed. There is nothing productive to do except wait.

I was grateful that there were many friends and family members praying. Oh God, please help us, is about the only prayer I could whisper.

It doesn't matter the words we say. God hears them all.

I surrender my fears to God:

_____

_____

_____

_____

_____

_____

_____

_____

_____

_____

_____

_____

_____

_____

_____

_____

_____

So do not fear; for I am with you; do not be dismayed; for I am your God. I will strengthen you and help you; I will uphold you with my righteous right hand. Isaiah 41:10 (NIV)

Standing in Faith

There was a large family camped out in the waiting room. They were disruptive and noisy. The television blared and the kids cried for attention. The waiting room was a mess. Food cartons, blankets, sleeping bags were scattered everywhere. It was impossible to find a quiet spot to sit or think or rest. I was irritated and resentful.

I overheard them talking one day. They were disagreeing about whether to turn off life support for their family member. They were waiting for death to take their loved one.

Sometimes life can cause disruption and noise and often there are too many things calling for our attention. The frustration of not being able to control anything is simply exhausting. We are left to rely on our faith, hope, and God's unlimited love.

Today I stand in faith.

Where can I let go today?

The thief comes only to steal and kill and destroy; I have come that they may have life, and have it to the full. John 10:10 (NIV)

Visualizing Love

It was shocking and disappointing to see tubes and wires surrounding my beloved husband.

I decided to see every tube and wire filled with love and light and all the prayers being sent as beams of love into his body and especially his heart.

Love is the healing presence.

What can I see with eyes of love today?

And so we know and rely on the love God has for us. 1 John 4:16 (NIV)

Medicine Comes from God

There are those who are afraid to take medicine and there are those who take it all too frequently. We found the best way to take medicine is with a dose of gratitude. Our constant prayer was that we would be guided to the best avenue for healing.

We prayed each day that God's presence was in the doctors, nurses, medications, tests, treatments. We thanked God each day for everything provided.

Thank you God.

What places can I recognize God's presence?

The Lord is my rock, my fortress and my deliverer; my God is my rock, in whom I take refuse. Psalm 18:2 (NIV)

Change is Constant

Whatever challenge we face as a caregiver on Monday, by Friday we are sure to have a new one.

In the life of a caregiver, change is constant. One worry or thought can take up all our time and energy, only to find that in 24 hours there is a new problem or concern.

I often found comfort in The Serenity Prayer:

God grant me the serenity

to accept the things I cannot change;

courage to change the things I can;

and wisdom to know the difference.

Where am I willing to receive God's wisdom?

I will instruct and teach you in the way you should go;
I will counsel you and watch over you. Psalm 32:8 (NIV)

Asking Questions

One of the challenges I noticed for myself was that I did not ask enough questions. What is the doctor's diagnosis? Why is there a new drug? What are the effects of a new drug? What changes can we expect to see?

I was not always able to be at the hospital when the doctors made rounds. When I arrived I would ask for an update and to see the doctor. The more information I had, the better equipped I was to make decisions.

I was grateful for guidance on the spiritual plane, which supported me in my decision-making on the physical plane.

What questions would I like answers to?

And I will pray the Father, and He will give you another Helper, that He may
abide with you forever. John 14:16 (NKJV)

Realization of Loss

An illness in the family changes everything. Normal everyday activities and tasks are set aside to care for a loved one.

Worry and fear are constant reminders that life is no longer the same. It takes a shift in attitude and energy to cope with the changes.

Life dramatically changes with illness. The caregiver feels the profound loss of a partner, a parent, a friend. We become aware of a loss of freedom and peace.

Time to reach out for prayer.

I acknowledge the changes in my life.

_____

_____

_____

_____

_____

_____

_____

_____

_____

_____

_____

_____

_____

_____

_____

I know the plans I have for you declares the Lord, plans to prosper you and not harm you, plans to give you hope and a future. Jeremiah 29:11 (NIV)

Back to the Basics

Things we take so much for granted are enormous tasks when dealing with an illness. Often after a serious illness the patient has to regain their strength. The simple things that we take for granted like eating, walking and going to the bathroom can be overwhelming for the patient.

The caregiver may appear to take it all in stride as we acknowledge and celebrate each success along the way. But the pain of watching the change can be overwhelming.

It is so important to acknowledge our grief and sense of loss. It is the most powerful way to move through it.

Today I am letting go…

_____

_____

_____

_____

_____

_____

_____

_____

_____

_____

_____

_____

_____

_____

_____

_____

Cast all your anxiety on Him because He cares for you. 1 Peter 5:7 (NIV)

The Economics of Illness

I am so grateful that we had planned for our future. A few years earlier we prepared our wills, power of attorney, and advance directive. Most of us resist thinking about illness and death and neglect to take action.

It is so important to have a plan before a crisis. Having to make major decisions during an illness or emergency adds to the overwhelm.

Praise God for guidance.

I accept clarity in the following financial matters:

_____

_____

_____

_____

_____

_____

_____

_____

_____

_____

_____

_____

_____

_____

_____

_____

*My God will meet all your needs according to his glorious riches in Christ
Jesus. Philippians 4:19 (NIV)*

No Small Steps

After an illness we learn to celebrate the small steps. Learning to walk, hold utensils, or reclaiming old memories are reasons to celebrate.

There are no small steps in God. Every step is a blessing. Each step reminds us of the preciousness of life.

We give all glory to God for the daily blessings.

I give thanks to God for the blessings in my life.

_____

_____

_____

_____

_____

_____

_____

_____

_____

_____

_____

_____

_____

_____

_____

_____

Delight yourself in the Lord, and he will give you the desires of your heart.
Psalm 37:4 (NIV)

Speech Therapy

Part of the speech therapist's responsibility is to make sure a stroke patient can swallow before they begin to eat solid food.

Laurence's speech therapist, Katie, made it her personal mission to make sure Laurence was able to eat. She arrived early each morning to his room and helped him eat breakfast.

I watched her amazing patience while she fed him. She smiled, laughed, and celebrated each bite with him. She took her time and waited as he swallowed.

When it was my turn to help him eat I was dismayed at my impatience and short attention span. Every bite felt like an eternity. Laurence's mind would wander off and he would forget to swallow. I would try to give him the next bite before he was finished. I felt so guilty as my patience was tested.

Fortunately, I realized that it was time to call for help. Our spiritual community showed up with infinite love, patience, and caring, and helped Laurence as he relearned to eat and speak. They thanked me a million times for letting them spend time with Laurence. They acted as if I did them a favor.

Caregiving is not necessarily about being the one to do everything. The great gift is opening the door to let others in so they can give.

Where can I let others in to support me?

_____

_____

_____

_____

_____

_____

_____

_____

_____

_____

_____

_____

_____

_____

_____

_____

_____

The Lord is good, a refuge in times of trouble. He cares for those who trust in him. Nahum 1:7 (NIV)

Unexpected Gifts

"You need to take care of yourself."

After the first twenty-five times, it was difficult to hear that statement without getting angry. Well-meaning friends didn't quite know what else to say. I tried to explain to each one of them, "You have no idea what I am going through!"

I was already feeling guilty for the thousands of things that I didn't do or couldn't do or didn't have time for. I heard the well-meaning suggestion as one more thing I should be doing.

I learned to take a moment to breathe. I remembered the unexpected gifts I had received. I felt incredibly grateful to the friends who helped me take care of myself: treated me to a facial, massage, and pedicure. They dropped off bubble bath and body lotion, home-cooked dinners and groceries. They sent cards, letters and thousands of prayers.

I realized the bottom line is all love.

I am so grateful God is so gracious.

What am I willing to receive today?

Every good and perfect gift is from above, coming down from the Father of heavenly lights. James 1:17 (NIV)

Beams of Love

I filled the bulletin board in Laurence's room with current photos and cards. Occasionally, Laurence was moved from one room to another. The nursing staff always took great care to transfer his precious photos to his new room and post them on the board.

I had an insight when opening his Father's Day card from his son Jason. Children open cards hoping to see money inside: grandparents open cards hoping to see photos of their grandchildren!

The photos on the bulletin board brought love and joy, hope and gratitude. The hospital staff asked questions and learned family member's names.

They say a picture is worth a thousand words. I say a photo sends a million beams of love.

I am willing to receive love today.

_____

_____

_____

_____

_____

_____

_____

_____

_____

_____

_____

_____

_____

_____

_____

He has taken me to the banquet hall, and his banner over me is love.
Song of Songs 2:4 (NIV)

Treats

The hospital staff members who treat our loved ones are amazing angels.

Many of them were humble, shy, and all of them hard-working and dedicated. It can be a challenge to find new ways to say thank you.

When friends asked what they could do, I asked for treats. Cookies, brownies, cupcakes, and other goodies were donated and graciously received by the staff.

A simple gift of a homemade treat was a blessing for the giver and the receiver.

What support am I willing to ask for?

Look to the Lord and his strength; seek his face always.
1 Chronicles 16:11 (NIV)

Pain Relief

Anyone caring for a loved one will testify to the ordeal of watching your loved one live with pain.

What is your pain level on a scale of 1 – 10? If Laurence answered it was a 4, I knew most likely it was a 9. He had a very high tolerance for pain.

Many patients don't realize they don't have to live with pain. Often the fear of taking medication is more debilitating than the pain. They suffer out of fear.

While the patient has physical pain, the caregiver is in emotional pain. The heart aches. The head throbs. Yet we persist and hold on to the vision of wholeness.

Thank goodness that prayer is the number-one pain reliever.

What pain am I willing to acknowledge and release?

For I am the Lord, your God, who takes hold of your right hand and says to you, Do not fear; I will help you. Jeremiah 33:3 (NIV)

Army of Angels

I realized one night after a long day at the hospital that Laurence had an army of people watching over him day and night. Because I had been feeling so very alone, I was moved and grateful for this blessing.

As a caregiver there are so many life or death decisions to make, a household to maintain, and finances to manage. There were many offers to help, but ultimately, decisions are made alone.

I was grateful to remember I had an army of angels watching over me. I was grateful to remember that I was not alone.

I walk this walk in faith.

I give thanks and bless the angels and loved ones supporting me.

_____

_____

_____

_____

_____

_____

_____

_____

_____

_____

_____

_____

_____

_____

_____

Praise him, all his angels; praise him, all his heavenly hosts.
Psalm 148:2 (NIV)

Trust

Laurence did not want to eat. No matter what we said or did to persuade him, he was not interested in food. I asked our friends to help and we all coaxed, prodded, and urged him to eat something.

One day his doctor mentioned that in this stage of his treatment, it is normal not to feel hungry or be interested in food. I felt like I had failed. Laurence was listening to his body. But I wasn't listening to him.

I realized all the fears connected with eating and how often we don't trust ourselves. Eating too much will lead to overeating. Not eating enough can lead to illness or death.

It's normal for a caregiver to feel that we've somehow failed our loved one. We rely on God's love to guide us.

Where will I trust God today?

Trust in the Lord with all your heart and lean not on your own understanding. Proverbs 3:5 (NIV)

Gratitude

As caregiver, I watched and learned. I developed patience and learned compassion. I deepened in gratitude.

I am so grateful to all those who sent emails, cards, prayers and good thoughts.

I also heard so many stories of faith. There was an ailment that seemed to have no cure and suddenly there was healing. Family struggles seemed hopeless, when love showed up to bring unity. There was loss that was devastating when someone arrived to help.

Walking this spiritual journey, we are aware of experiences that may frustrate, confuse, disappoint and discourage. In those darkest moments we turn to find gratitude and renewed faith.

Faith keeps us going, for we know that, "This, too, shall pass."

I am so grateful for these blessings in my life:

In all your ways acknowledge him and he will make your paths straight.
Proverbs 3:6 (NIV)

Navigator

Laurence was at one hospital for about thirty days and then transferred to another for rehabilitation. About twenty days later he was transferred back to cancer hospital for a few days and then back to rehab. After about a week, he was transferred again—you get the picture.

I was always grateful that God was my navigator and personal GPS system. Faith guided me and grace protected me on my journey.

I am grateful for God's guidance today.

_____

_____

_____

_____

_____

_____

_____

_____

_____

_____

_____

_____

_____

_____

_____

_____

_____

You will make known to me the path of life; In Your presence is fullness of joy; In Your right hand there are pleasures forever. Psalm 16:11 (NASB)

Be Kind to Caregivers

I ran into a friend at the grocery store one day. I finished giving her an update and she commented on how tired I looked.

I have never understood how telling someone they look tired is helping them. Maybe if she had said, "You look tired, let me help you out with your groceries? Can I run some errands for you? Can I buy you a cup of coffee?"

A caregiver has little time for personal care. Life is about doctors, medicine and insurance, paying bills and answering questions. Most of the time caregivers find it difficult to focus on a topic, remember an appointment, or find their car in the hospital parking lot. We already know we look exhausted, worried, stressed, and frazzled.

Please be kind to caregivers. Please find something uplifting to say. "You have a lot of courage." "I am amazed at how you get things done." "I am impressed with your patience."

I speak for all of us and say we greatly appreciate your kindness.

I acknowledge my many strengths.

_____

_____

_____

_____

_____

_____

_____

_____

_____

_____

_____

_____

_____

_____

_____

_____

Beloved, let us love one another, for love is from God, and whoever loves has been born of God and knows God. 1 John 4:7 (NIV)

Faith

Every day is different in a patient's life. A patient can wake up to find an updated drug protocol, a revised schedule, and new tests. Change is constant. The only thing to rely on is faith.

No two people develop their faith the same way. I have found that faith is one part willingness, two parts surrender, and three parts gratitude. Faith is the willingness to receive without dictating the steps, letting go without anxiety, and living in a state of gratitude.

When we live in faith, we learn to live in gratitude for the process, the practice, and the patience.

I place my faith in God today.

_____

_____

_____

_____

_____

_____

_____

_____

_____

_____

_____

_____

_____

_____

_____

_____

For we walk by faith, not by sight. 2 Corinthians 5:7 (NIV)

A Caregiver's Prayer

My heart and mind are open to accept God's unlimited presence of love. I know love moves into the very cells of my being bringing light, harmony and peace.

I ask for guidance as I go about serving those loved ones around me. I know that wisdom guides my decisions, love expresses through my words and grace steers my actions.

I invite God's healing presence of Love to wash away any doubt or fear. It is love that I welcome and embrace into my life.

I enter this day with a grateful heart and receive the blessings love has in store for me. Amen.

Lord, hear my prayer...

Do not be anxious about anything, but in everything, by prayer and petition, with thanksgiving, present your requests to God.
Philippians 4:4-6 (NIV)

Worry

On Monday, Laurence slept all day. I worried that he was sleeping so long.

On Wednesday, his nurse told me he wasn't sleeping through the night. I worried and wondered why he was awake.

On Thursday, Laurence was sedated to prepare for a test he needed. I worried about the test outcome.

By Friday, I was exhausted.

Worry takes time, energy, and keeps caregivers in fear. Whenever possible it is good to take attention off the appearances in the world and turn our awareness to God.

I turn my awareness to God today.

I will wait with hope and expectancy for the God of my salvation; my God will hear me. Micah 7:7 (AMP)

Letting Go

I remember catching butterflies as a child. I learned how to hold tightly to the wings—but not too tightly, so as not to crush them. I learned to let go and watch the butterfly fly away.

As a caregiver, I am learning to let go and let God.

What am I willing to let go of today?

Come to me, all you who are weary and burdened, and I will give you rest.
Matthew 11:28 (NIV)

Move Mountains

Sometimes one ailment seems to disappear while another takes hold. It feels like one step forward, three steps back.

A friend reminded me of the scripture from Matthew 17:20:

"I tell you the truth. If you have faith as small as a mustard seed, you can say to this mountain, 'Move from here to there' and it will move. Nothing will be impossible for you."

The power of faith.

Where I am willing to deepen my faith?

Your word is a lamp unto my feet and a light for my path.
Psalm 119:105 (NIV)

Expectations

One of the first things I realized I had to let go of as a caregiver was my expectation. Of everything.

I realized it's all about attachment. The difference between expectation and expectancy is attachment. Expectation has us hoping and wishing that what we want will show up. Expectancy motivates us to look for the good in life. Expectations keep us waiting while expectancy encourages patience.

Expectation comes from the mind and expectancy comes from the soul. The more attached I am, the more restricted life seems to be. If I let go of attachment, I open up the realm of opportunity.

I release my expectations and open to the expectancy of God's love.

Where am I willing to release my attachment?

Our light and momentary troubles are achieving for us an eternal glory that far outweighs them all. 2 Corinthians 4:17 (NIV)

Never Alone

Spiritual faith is knowing that I don't walk this journey alone. When I turn my awareness to God I know something greater is supporting me in my efforts and on my journey. As I develop the awareness of something greater than what I can see, I see more dramatic results.

I know as I am grounded I am in faith, I am able to meet the challenges that show up.

I am truly grateful for my awareness of faith, God's love and the extraordinary blessings in my life.

I recognize that I am never alone.

So faith comes from hearing, and hearing through the word of God.
Romans 10:8 (NIV)

Bible References

The scriptures used in the book were obtained from one of the following translations:

AMP   Amplified Bible

MSG   The Message Bible

NASB   New American Standard Bible

NIV   New International Version

NKJV   New King James Version

More information about bible translations can be found:

Biblios: bible.cc

Bible Gateway: www.biblegateway.com

Caregiving Resources

Below are just a few of the books and websites I have found. Visit my website for the online version of this page and links to the resources.

www.sacredheartministries.org/services/caregivingresources

Books

Berman, Claire, Caring for Yourself While Caring for your Aging Parents: How to Help, How to Survive, Holt Paperbacks, 2001

Meyers, Maria and Paula Deer, The Comfort of Home: An Illustrated Step by Step Guide for Caregivers, Caretrust Publications, 2006

Sheehy, Gail, *Passages in Caregiving*, William Morrow, 2010

Jacobs, Barry, The Emotional Survival Guide for Caregivers, The Guildford Press, 2006

Caregiving Organizations

Well Spouse Association: www.wellspouse.org

National Family Caregivers Association: www.nfcacares.org

National Alliance for Caregiving: www.caregiving.org/

Caregiving Websites

www.caregiver.com

www.caring.com

www.caregiving.com

Medical Information

WebMD: www.webmd.com

Health Central: www.healthcentral.com

AARP: www.aarp.com

Care Central: www.carecentral.com

About the Author

Christine Green is a published author, professional speaker and teacher. She is an ordained minister and founder of Sacred Heart Ministries in Portland, Oregon, providing global resources and education for spiritual evolution.

Rev. Christine has served in leadership roles at a number of ministries both in California and Oregon. She has had the opportunity to teach, facilitate and counsel others for over 20 years both nationally and abroad. Her areas of professional interest include nurturing women to live from an empowered sense of self, teaching spiritual tools and practices, caring for the caregiver, and the power of purpose.

She is the author of Anatomy of Caring; Insights on faith from a caregiver and a patient and Authentic Spirituality; A Woman's Guide to Living an Empowered Life.

Contact her at revgreen@sacredheartministries.org. Learn more on her website: www.sacredheartministries.org.

Made in the USA
Charleston, SC
28 June 2013